# The One Hour Bookkeeper's

# How to Do a Year's Worth of Bookkeeping in One Day

## A Step-By-Step Guide to QuickBooks for Small Businesses

By E.T. Barton and Robin E. Davis

How to Do a Year's Worth of Bookkeeping in One Day

By E.T. Barton        &        Robin E. Davis

By E.T. Barton      &      Robin E. Davis

How to Do a Year's Worth of Bookkeeping in One Day

By E.T. Barton       &       Robin E. Davis

## **Other Products by E.T. Barton, Robin E. Davis or the OneHourBookkeeper.com website:**

### THE ONE HOUR BOOKKEEPING METHOD:

How to Do Your Books in One Hour or Less

### HOW TO START A LUCRATIVE

### VIRTUAL BOOKKEEPING BUSINESS:

A Step-by-Step Guide to Working Less and Making More

in the Bookkeeping Industry

### 10 WAYS TO SAVE MONEY ON

### BOOKKEEPING & ACCOUNTING

### DIARY OF A BAD, BAD BOOKKEEPER

A Cautionary Embezzlement Tale

for Small Business Owners Everywhere

~ v ~

# Thank You for Purchasing

## "HOW TO DO A YEAR'S WORTH OF BOOKKEEPING IN ONE DAY"
### A Step-by-Step Guide for Small Businesses

I want to make this process as easy for you as possible. As such, I have downloaded many of the checklists in a Printable PDF Form at this link:

www.OneHourBookkeeper.com/aywbonuses

Also, due to printing costs for color versions being too high, this book is in black and white. *However, you can find color versions of the tables at the same website.* Simply pop on over and download your free worksheets so you can start checking off all of your "Must-Do's" Today.

Thanks Again,

—E.T. Barton

*This EBook is owned by E.T. Barton and Robin Davis, the bloggers of www.OneHourBookkeeper.com.*

How to Do a Year's Worth of Bookkeeping in One Day

By E.T. Barton      &      Robin E. Davis

How to Do a Year's Worth of Bookkeeping in One Day

By E.T. Barton      &      Robin E. Davis

# Table of Contents

~ x ~

How to Do a Year's Worth of Bookkeeping in One Day

By E.T. Barton         &         Robin E. Davis

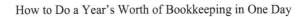

How to Do a Year's Worth of Bookkeeping in One Day

By E.T. Barton      &      Robin E. Davis

# INTRODUCTION

## *What This Book is NOT*

This book is *not* a replacement for a day-to-day Bookkeeper. It does not discuss Accounts Receivable, Accounts Payable, Payroll Procedures, or Tax Reports of any kind. It is not about writing checks, making deposits, or dealing with money. It is not meant to replace day-to-day Bookkeeping Data Entry in any way, shape or form.

## *The Mission of This Book*

Now that you know what this book is *not*, I'll tell you why this book was written. This book was written for small businesses who may

~ 1 ~

not be up to date on their bookkeeping, or that may never have done any bookkeeping. It is written for Small Business Owners (SBOs) who have no bookkeeper and need to enter their own bookkeeping data entry, or for bookkeepers who may be behind and need some ideas on getting caught up fast. It is written with the assumption that the reader has little or no QuickBooks knowledge, so it may bore those who already know the program inside and out. This book is all about fast, dirty, no-holds barred data entry that will get a small business's books up-to-date as quickly as possible so that an accountant can do the business's taxes in a timely fashion. (In that vein, it will also work for anyone who needs to get their income and expenses ready quickly for their personal taxes.) By the time you are done with this book, you will have an up-to-date set of business books that you can continue to use in the following years.

## *What You Need to Use This Book:*

In order to use this book, you must have QuickBooks. It does not matter what version of QuickBooks, just that you have QuickBooks. Although there are many bookkeeping programs available today that can do a company's books, in the opinion of the authors, QuickBooks is the best by far. It is one of the only programs that can "talk" to your bank / credit card accounts and download those accounts' details into an easy-to-post file. It is also one of very few programs out there *not* designed for bookkeepers, but for everyday users. The first fact will make data entry fast and easy, while the latter will mean that anyone can do what this book teaches.

**IF YOU DO NOT HAVE QUICKBOOKS, you can actually download the Simple Start version of QuickBooks and try it for free for 30 days.** If you plan it right, you could download the free sample, do your Day's Worth of Work, and then submit all the paperwork to your accountant *without buying the program.* However, I'm pretty sure that once you do buy the program, you will want to keep it. Especially because you can do this 12-Step Program year after year and thus keep your business's taxes up-to-date.

*Quick Note: A free version of QuickBooks Simple Start is available at the Intuit QuickBooks website:*

*http://quickbooks.intuit.com/product/accounting-software/free-accounting-software.jsp.*

## *What Your Accountant Will Expect From You Before Doing Your Company's Taxes:*

Wondering what your Accountant or Tax Man might want from you to do your taxes (whether for Small Business or Personal taxes)? Here's a list of commonly asked for items:

Personal Income Tax Returns:

- A copy of your prior year tax return (if using a new tax preparer or CPA)

Income:

- 1099's (Interest, Retirement, IRA distributions, Pensions, Social Security, Unemployment, Dividends, Stock/Bond Sales, State Income Tax Refund, etc.)
- W-2 forms (wages)

Expenses:

- Educator expenses
- Tuition
- Health savings account deposits

- Child care expenses, including name and Tax ID # of Child Care Provider
- Moving expenses
- Student loan interest
- Schedule A - 1098-Mortgage Interest Statement, property taxes, medical & dental expenses, motor vehicle taxes (copy of DMV bills), both cash and non-cash donations (include name of charity and amount or value of donation), un-reimbursed employee expenses, and tax preparation fees (for 2008 returns).
- If you purchased a home in 2009, provide a copy of your HUD-1 or closing statement.

## Business Income Tax Returns/Schedule C:

- A copy of your prior year business tax return (if using a new tax preparer or CPA)
- All 1099-Misc's received as an Independent Contractor, Partnership or LLC
- Copies of all 1099s/1096 distributed to independent contractors you PAID
- W-2 & W-3 forms and Quarterly Payroll reports for wages PAID by your business

- Payroll Summary for the year
- Any other Quarterly Tax reports (Sales & Use tax, etc.)
- December's Yearend and January's current bank statements & reconciliation reports
- The Petty Cash or Cash on Hand balance and reconciliation report
- Credit Card statements and total finance charges for the year
- List of Inventory and Assets, including any NEWLY purchased assets
- Mileage records
- Home business office information (total. Sq. footage of home & of the home office, mortgage payments or rent, annual insurance and utility costs)
- A detailed printout of any draws, investments or payroll information on partners or shareholders
- Health insurance paid by the company for the owners/partners
- Year End financial statements: Balance Sheet, Profit and Loss Statement & Trial Balance
- A copy or backup of the company's automated accounting data file if you use one (QuickBooks, Peach Tree, MYOB, etc.)

- If you haven't recorded your business transactions throughout the year, provide copies of the entire year's bank and credit card statements.

This list is not intended to be "all inclusive", but rather a guide or quick reference to the forms and documents most commonly requested by a tax preparer or CPA. Many tax preparers and CPA's will provide you with a checklist of the documents needed to prepare your tax return. In addition, many use a questionnaire to obtain information and/or determine any changes that may have occurred over the prior year (your filing status [got married, divorced], dependents [had or adopted a child], if sold or purchased property [primary or secondary residence, rental property, stocks or bonds, etc.]).

*Just a Thought: You may want to consider hiring an independent bookkeeper to record your accounting transactions, and reconcile your bank and credit card statements for the year. Accountants and CPA's often employ bookkeepers to handle this task for them and charge a much higher rate for the service than you'll pay an independent bookkeeper directly.*

## *If You Don't Plan to Use an Accountant:*

If you have no intention of hiring an accountant to do your small business taxes, and you are a sole proprietor or a very small business, it is the recommendation of the authors that you use the information in this book to get your bookkeeping up to date, and then purchase the TurboTax Deluxe program in order to file your taxes. *While it is always a good idea to use an accountant or tax preparer to make sure you are doing your taxes correctly*, we understand that the high cost of hiring a professional can often be a deterrent. The Deluxe edition of TurboTax is the edition for small businesses, and since it was created by Intuit (the parent company of QuickBooks), it easily communicates with QuickBooks and posts the majority of what you need posted to the corresponding tax categories in your tax forms. It will also walk you step-by-step through an interview process that can help you fill in the rest of the holes.

**Important Note**: *If you have stocks that need to be reported, you will also want to purchase Quicken. QuickBooks does not really deal with day-to-day stock purchases, while Quicken can quickly download all stock purchases and sales, and will also drop the information easily into TurboTax Deluxe.*

# CHAPTER 1:

# Getting Prepared

# What You Need Before You Begin

To enter your books quickly, you'll need to be organized. You have to have everything in a proper order before you sit down at your desk so that you can be efficient when doing your data entry. If you aren't organized, one day's entry can quickly turn into a week, and then a month... and then you're late. So, be sure to have the following items all together and in order before you move on to **CHAPTER 2: GETTING DOWN TO THE NITTY GRITTY.**

## ITEM # 1:  Have QuickBooks Downloaded and Your Company Information Already Set Up, Including Check Registers and Credit Card Registers.

If you've used QuickBooks before, then you have probably already been taken care of this step.  You should have probably already gone through the step-by-step interview process and entered all your company's information regarding location, tax IDs, and which chart of accounts will be used.  You've probably also set up checking accounts and credit card accounts in QuickBooks.

If you haven't set up QuickBooks, then do that now.  As soon as you click "Create A New Company", QuickBooks EasyStep Interview screen will pop up and walk you through everything the Program needs in order to do your bookkeeping.  *Be sure to have your Federal Employer Identification Number or Social Security Number ready, since you will want to input this in the interview step.*

## ITEM # 2:  Make Sure You Have Online Access to Your Bank Accounts and Credit Card Accounts.

If you haven't already taken advantage of your bank's online account access, go NOW and sign up for it.  This is one of the best free tools any SBO can use to track their money. If you have a bookkeeper, it is also a good idea to occasionally log on and make sure everything looks good in the account... that items are being paid in a timely fashion and that your bank account is not in the red. But most importantly, you will also need this later on in the Data Entry process.

Once you've created online access to your bank account, do the same with your credit cards.

## ITEM # 3: Check with Your Bank to See if Your Bank Account Information Can Be Downloaded.

*(This Step is <u>Incredibly Important</u> and often <u>Time Sensitive</u>, so make sure you do it IMMEDIATELY. The longer you wait, the more data entry you will have to do. Trust me for now... you'll understand more in CHAPTER 2.)*

As stated in the Introduction, QuickBooks is one of the best bookkeeping programs out there because it can "talk" to your bank account. As of the publication of this book, hundreds of banks already are able to create a **"Web Connect" file or an "IIF File"** that can be dropped into your Company's QuickBooks program. Some banks (like Bank of America) are able to download as many as 11 months of bank transactions, while others (like Chase) will only allow you to download approximately 4 months of transactions. Still, there are many banks out there (usually small local banks) that **cannot** work with QuickBooks or any other bookkeeping program. That is why you will want to check with your bank immediately to see if they offer *"downloadable files for QuickBooks"* through their online banking. (If your bank doesn't offer online banking at all... you're at the wrong bank. Switch immediately. *And if they don't offer downloadable files for QuickBooks, it is an excellent idea to switch to one that does right away regardless of your history with the bank.* What you have to take into consideration is that the banks that don't offer these services mean higher bookkeeping fees – *period*.)

If your bank does NOT offer downloadable files for QuickBooks, move on to **ITEM # 4**.

If your bank DOES offer these files, then do the following:
1. Login to your online business bank account.
2. Go into the checking account you use for your business.
3. Find the "Download" link and click on it. The "Download" link should look something like this:

How to Do a Year's Worth of Bookkeeping in One Day

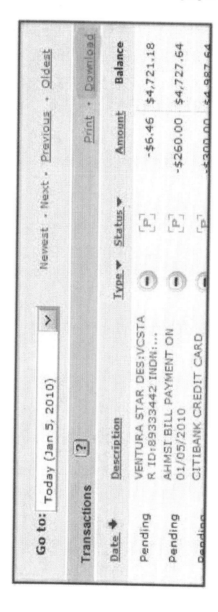

By E.T. Barton      &      Robin E. Davis

Once you've clicked on the Download link, you will be taken to a page that will show you different download options. The page should look something like this:

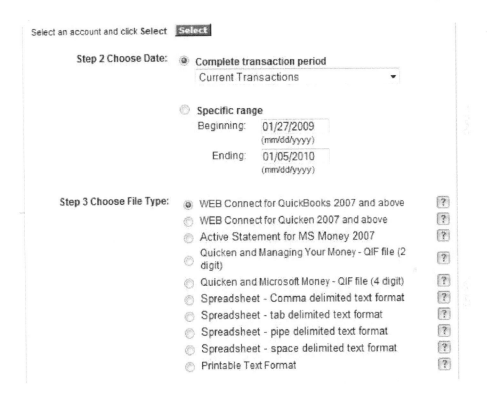

Usually, whatever dates are shown on this page are the maximum number of days (and months) that your bank will allow you to download your transactions into a bookkeeping program.

4. On the download page, choose the widest date range possible – and do it **TODAY**. *The longer you wait to do this step, the more transactions you will lose and the more transactions you will have to enter manually later on.*

5. Click "Download" or "Save File." Save this file to your desktop as a "Web Connect" or an "IIF File" so you can easily find it later.

6. Done. That's it.

7. Now repeat these steps for other business bank accounts and for business credit card accounts. Again – the sooner the better.

8. Also, check with your Merchant Account banks to find out if they offer downloadable transactions into QuickBooks. *(If PayPal is the Merchant Account you use to accept credit card payments, they DO offer downloadable QuickBooks Files.)*

## ITEM # 4:  Get All Your Bank Statements and Put Them in Sequential Order by Month.

If you cannot find your bank statements, or aren't sure you have them all, you can usually download bank statements directly from your bank account's online access. Download them all to a folder on your desktop, and you can ditch the hard copies altogether. This way, if you

~ 15 ~

ever get audited, you can quickly and easily reprint them from your computer instead of having to go through filing cabinets to find them.

Once you have downloaded the statements, print them out and put them in order by month.

## ITEM # 5: Highlight All Repetitive Transactions on Your Bank Statements

Technically, you don't have to go through ALL of your bank statements in this step to find all the transactions that repeat because when items repeat, they usually do so all year long. So, if they show up on one statement, they will show up again and again on other statements. However, if you DO highlight all the transactions that repeat on ALL bank statements, you will be less likely to "accidentally" enter them later on.

Therefore, go ahead and grab all of your bank statements for the year and scan quickly through them. If anything repeats and is month after month and is the same amount each month (like car payments, rent, monthly website fees, monthly checking fees, etc.), then highlight those items now. (We will go over "the why" of this step in CHAPTER 2 – Step 4.)

Once you're done, return those statements to the stack and continue on.

## ITEM # 6:  Get a Credit Card Business Expense Report, if Available.  If it is NOT Available, Organize All Credit Card Statements in Sequential Order by Month.

Many business credit cards now offer year-end Expense Reports that categorize all purchases made by the type of expense.  (It might also be known as an Annual Statement of Charges.)  If you can get the credit card company to give you these reports, you will save *at least* an hour of data entry.  If you cannot get these reports, or your credit card does not offer them, then you can also download credit card statements to your desktop from online access.  Download these statements to a folder on your desktop as well.  Just like the bank statements, you can ditch the hard copies and keep digital copies for any potential audits.

Once you have downloaded the statements, print them out and put them in order by month.  Set these aside for later.

*For Future Reference:   American Express automatically generates this report every year for its clients.  So, if you don't have an American Express card, you may want to consider getting one.*

## ITEM # 7:  Get Your Check Register, if You Kept One.

If you use your debit card more than you write checks... that is FABULOUS!  You will have a lot less data entry to do than another SBO who writes checks.

If you write checks more than you use your debit card, then your check register and returned checks are going to be the only way for you to accurately enter and post the payments you made to their corresponding expense accounts.  A Check Register is the fastest, easiest way to do this.

## ITEM # 8:  Organize All Hardcopies of Checks into Sequential Order.

Let's face it:  SBOs don't always have time to record debits and credits in a register.  Nor do they always remember to do it when they get back to the office.  So, if you don't have an accurately filled-in check register, you *will* need hardcopies of the checks you wrote. These usually come with your returned bank statements, and you will need to put them in sequential *numerical* order (NOT by date) so that when you do your data entry, the data entry will be easier.  If the hard copies of the checks are not returned with your statements, then copies

~ 18 ~

of the checks should be included with the PDF statements you download from your bank.

*Quick Note: Any checks that are missing could mean one of three things: 1) The check has not cleared the bank yet; 2) the Check has been voided, lost or thrown away; or 3) the check was destroyed to hide embezzlement. Whether you're worried about embezzlement or not, putting your checks in sequential order is a good way to make sure everything has been done the way it should have been. It also provides you with an opportunity to review all of your cleared checks at once and look for who signed the check, and who endorsed it.*

## ITEM # 9: If You Accept Credit Cards for Payment (and Can't Download a Full Year's Worth of Transactions), You Will Need Your Monthly Merchant Account Statements.

Merchant Accounts are all different, so your company may or may not offer downloadable files or online access. Find out from your Merchant Account Bank if they have downloadable PDF Statements. If they do, you can save them digitally and print out hard copies (for data entry or for audits). If they don't, you will need to find the hard copies now.

Put them in order by month and set aside for later.

## ITEM # 10:  Tally Up Your Sales

In CHAPTER 2 - STEP 9, you will have to decide exactly how you want to enter your sales.  You can either enter in 365 daily sales entries, or you can enter sales entries from your bank statements.  Entering the sales from your bank statements means A LOT LESS data entry (and thus saves more time).  But, if you plan on analyzing the sales of one day to the same day in following years, you will want to have daily tallies of your sales.  You can either get this from cash register tapes (which will have the balances totaled for you ahead of time), or you can tally them up yourself from daily receipts.

If you think you'd rather have the most accurate sales totals possible, but you do not have cash register receipts... then this Item is going to be very important for you.  Begin by finding all your sales receipts and putting them in chronological order.  Staple together all receipts that were issued on the same day, and then write the total of those receipts on whichever receipt is on top.  By writing it in big bold numbers, you will save time in data entry later on.

*My recommendation, however... just go with the bank statements and skip this item altogether.*

## ITEM # 11:  Change Your QuickBooks Preferences to Save Time

Now that we have everything in order, it is time to turn QuickBooks into your own virtual bookkeeper.  To do this, simply login to your QuickBooks account, and then do the following:

1. Set Up Your Preferences In Order to Avoid Unnecessary Mistakes:  It's really easy to "accidentally" record items in QuickBooks if you aren't careful.  Therefore, to reduce the potential for making these time-consuming mistakes (time-consuming because you will have to find those items and delete / change them), we're going to Edit Your Preferences.  Do this by:

    a. Click on "Edit", then "Preferences".

    b. Go to the "General" Tab, then the "My Preferences" tab.

    c. Make sure the button that says "Pressing Enter Moves Between Fields" is selected.  Believe it or not, this one little box will save you hours of bookkeeping time trying to fix mistakes.

**d. Item C is the most important thing you can do to save time**, but here are a few more boxes you should check in order to make your QuickBooks friendlier and easier to use. Match your Preferences up to this screen.

(Go to www.OneHourBookkeeper.com/AYWBonsues for a printable version of these shortcuts.)

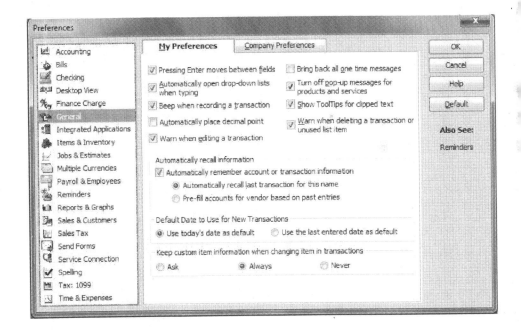

~ 22 ~

e. *Make sure* you check the box in the "Automatically recall information" area. This button will also save you tons of future data entry time.

f. Depending on YOUR preference, you may want to check the "Automatically place decimal point" box, but personally, *I would not.* I find that when I have it checked, I tend to make more mistakes that I then have to search for, find and fix – often because I can't remember if I entered enough digits or not. I find that I make fewer mistakes if I just plan to add the decimal from the beginning.

g. Now click on the Accounting Tab to the left and the "Company Preferences" tab at the top. The screen should look like this:

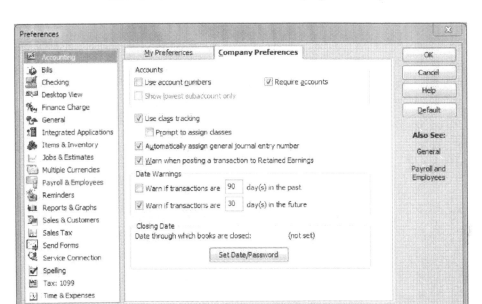

h. Change your warning preference so that you are NOT warned when "transactions are 90 days in the past." You're going to be entering things that ARE in the past, and you really don't want to have to keep closing the warning box.

i. Check the box so that you ARE warned when "transactions are 30 days in the future." This can save you tons of fixing since it is the inclination of QuickBooks to change the date to the current year if a year is not provided. So, to avoid accidentally posting transactions meant for last year in this year's file, this box is pretty important.

~ 24 ~

j. Match up your selections to the two screens above, and you should be good.

## ITEM # 12: Setup QuickBooks to Access Your Online Accounts

This is an important step that will help your QuickBooks program "talk" to your bank IN THE FUTURE. It can be useful now, but it is NOT NECESSARY. We are actually going to manually "force" QuickBooks to read your file. However, if you do want to create the Web Connection now, you can do so by:

1. Go to **"Banking"**, **"Online Banking"** and then **"Set up Account for Online Services."**

2. **Select the Check Register** (or credit card register) you are currently setting up in the drop down box and click **"Next."**

3. **Select the Name of your Bank** in the next drop down box and click **"Next."**

4. At this point, depending upon the bank, you will either be asked what type of connection you would like to make, or you will be asked if your bank has already activated online banking for QuickBooks. Just follow each of the steps QuickBooks offers until you get to the end.

- *(If you are unable to "Web Connect" with your bank, don't fret. You can still download your Web Connect Files or IIF files as detailed in Item # 3.)*

5. Repeat these steps for your other bank and credit card accounts. Again, if you are unable to fulfill any of the steps here for your bank or credit card, then forget it and we'll force it in manually.

That's it. You should now have completed or collected all of the items listed, and you are ready to get to the Nitty Gritty of bookkeeping... the data entry.

To reiterate, you must complete the following items before you can begin your Day's Worth of Data Entry:

# Quick-Step Checklist:

1. _____ QuickBooks Downloaded and Your Company Information Already Set Up

2. _____ Make Sure You Have Online Access to Your Bank Accounts and Credit Card Accounts.

3. _____ Check with Your Bank to See if Your Bank Account Information Can Be Downloaded.

4. _____ Get All Your Bank Statements and Put Them in Sequential Order by Month.

5. _____ Highlight All Repetitive Transactions on Your Bank Statements

6. _____ Get a Credit Card Business Expense Report, if Available. If it is NOT Available, Organize All Credit Card Statements in Sequential Order by Month.

7. _____ Get Your Check Register, if You Kept One.

8. _____ Organize All Hardcopies of Checks into Sequential Order.

9. _____ If You Accept Credit Cards for Payment (and Can't Download a Full Year's Worth of Transactions), You Will Need Your Monthly Merchant Account Statements.

10. _____ Tally Up Your Sales

11. _____ Change Your QuickBooks Preferences to Save Time

12. _____ Setup QuickBooks to Access Your Online Accounts

(Go to www.OneHourBookkeeper.com/AYWBonsues for a printable version of these shortcuts.)

# CHAPTER 2:

# Getting Down to the Nitty Gritty

# Your Day of Data Entry Has Now Begun

Welcome back.

I'm assuming if you're in this chapter, you are now ready to do your One Day's Worth of Bookkeeping. Your schedule should be cleared. Turn off your phone...don't even think about looking at your email...we're getting serious now.

If you haven't done so already, log into your QuickBooks account.

~ 29 ~

While your QuickBooks program is loading, here are some shortcut keys you should memorize before you get started. Get as familiar with them as you can... you'll be using them *a lot*.

---

## <u>Shortcuts that are the same in QuickBooks</u>

## <u>as they are in Excel and Word:</u>

- ***Tab*** = **Moves to the Next Data Entry Field**
- ***Shift*** + ***Tab*** = **Moves to the Previous Data Entry Field**
- ***Ctrl*** + ***Tab*** = **Moves to the next open window within the program**
- ***Ctrl*** + ***F*** = <u>**F**</u>**ind**

  (In QuickBooks, this shortcut will open a Find Box that will help you find transactions and mistakes.)
- ***Ctrl*** + ***C*** = <u>**C**</u>**opy**
- ***Ctrl*** + ***V*** = **Paste**
- ***Ctrl*** + ***P*** = <u>**P**</u>**rint**

<u>(Go to www.OneHourBookkeeper.com/AYWBonsues for a printable version of these shortcuts.)</u>

---

## QuickBooks Shortcuts:

- ***Ctrl + Enter* = "Save and New" / "Next" or "Okay"** (depending on the screen you're in; basically, *this is going to be your new best friend*, and the most used shortcut you can use).

- ***Ctrl + W* = <u>W</u>rite Checks** (This will be your *second* most used shortcut since you're about to do a lot of "check writing.")

- ***Ctrl + R* = <u>R</u>egister** (This will go to your default check register first, but you can also use it to select a register for ANYthing... customers, vendors, accounts, items, etc. This will be your *third* most used key.)

- ***Ctrl + D* = <u>D</u>elete** (If you're not familiar with QuickBooks, this shortcut may actually become your most used shortcut. This will delete anything you currently have open—check, invoice, sales receipt, etc.)

- ***Ctrl + M* = <u>M</u>emorize** (When you are in a transaction that you know is going to repeat itself monthly, weekly, bi-monthly, etc., then you're going to want to memorize the transaction. This way, QuickBooks will enter it automatically for you multiple times, thus saving you time.)

- ***Ctrl + H* = <u>H</u>istory** (This shortcut will help you find "Linked" Transactions. For example, if you are in a deposit and want to see if that deposit is "Linked" to a customer payment, you would use this shortcut to see the History associated with that transaction.)

(Go to www.OneHourBookkeeper.com/AYWBonsues for a printable version of these shortcuts.)

*Quick Note: For many people, using "the Alt Key" + "a corresponding underlined letter from the menu bar" + "a letter corresponding to the desired action" would be easier than using "Ctrl" + "One Letter" because it has been done in many other accounting programs, as well as Excel and Word. (For example, to print, you would go to Alt + F (for File) + P (for Print) to print instead of Ctrl + P.) So, if you are more familiar with the Alt Key commands and the Menu Bar, feel free to use those in lieu of the Ctrl commands. However, since this book was written expressly for people who are NOT familiar with QuickBooks, I am going to stick to the Ctrl Commands throughout the rest of this book.*

## *In Case of Mistakes*

If at any time you accidentally enter something wrong, or realize later that you expensed something to the wrong account, don't fret. Simply Press Ctrl + F to open the find screen. Use this screen to find the transaction (either name or amount), and you will see everything that matches that criteria in the bottom screen. Double click your transaction to open it and make your changes. It's that simple.

Here's how to "Find" and Correct Items step-by-step:

---

### To "Find" Any Transaction in QuickBooks

- "Find" the transaction by Pressing **Ctrl + F**. This will open the Find screen, which looks like this (in all versions of QuickBooks):

---

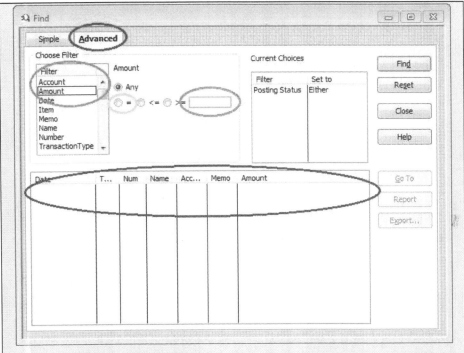

- **Click on the Advanced Tab** at the top (shown in red).

- **Select "Amount"** in the "Filter" box (shown in orange).

- **Click on the "=" sign** in the Amount Area (shown in yellow).

- **Enter the Amount** in the box (shown in green).

- Press *Ctrl + Enter* **(or "Find").**

- All Matching Transactions will show up in the bottom (as shown in blue).

- If you see your transaction, **double click it to open it**.

- Check to make sure all the information is correct and change anything that is not. Press *Ctrl + Enter* to save the transaction.

(Go to www.OneHourBookkeeper.com/AYWBonsues for a printable version of these shortcuts.)

If you don't see your transaction, **Click the "Reset" button** (on the left), then **choose a new Filter in the Filter box** (like Name, Date or Transaction Type).

If you still cannot find your transaction, it probably isn't entered. At this point, go ahead and re-enter the transaction according to the steps you will learn in this Chapter.

## MAKING QUICKBOOKS DO THE MAJORITY OF YOUR BOOKKEEPING

*(Quick Note: From here on out, all items in* **Bold** *are the* **Buttons /** **Actions** *you need to find and do to complete that step. All Items in* ***Italics AND Bold*** *will usually be the* ***Shortcut Keystrokes*** *you will want to do to complete that step even faster. Also, a quick reference box is at the end of each section to help you complete or repeat the steps even faster.)*

### STEP 1: Upload your Bank's Web Connect File into

~ 35 ~

## QuickBooks

Remember when you downloaded your Bank's Web Connect or IIF File back in CHAPTER 1 – Item # 3? Well, now is the time to upload that file into your QuickBooks account. As I stated earlier, this one little step is going to save you hours, days, even weeks of data entry. To upload it, you are going to do the following:

1. Go to **"File"**, **"Utilities"**, and then **"Import."**
2. **Select the <u>type</u> of file you downloaded from your bank –** either Web Connect Files or IIF Files. (If for some reason you do not see this option – maybe because you have an older version of QuickBooks – then go ahead and go to www.OneHourBookkeeper.com and email me with the problem you are having and what version of QuickBooks you are using. I will do what I can to help you with your version.)

3. QuickBooks will now open a browsing screen that will allow you to pick the file you downloaded from your bank. **Select the file and click "Okay."**

4. QuickBooks will instantly upload all of those transactions into your Online Banking register making them ready to post.

---

**Upload Your Bank File:**

**(All Versions of QuickBooks)**

- Go to "File"
- "Utilities"
- "Import"
- Find Your "Web Connect" or "IIF" File and Select it.
- Click "Okay"

         - Done!

---

That's it. You are now ready to post hundreds – even thousands – of transactions in minutes.

## STEP 2: Post Your "Web Connect" / "IIF" Files to the Appropriate Accounts.

Now that your bank file has been uploaded, the next step is to post these transactions to your bank account. Before I tell you how to do that, there is one thing you must understand: <u>QuickBooks can add MULTIPLE transactions to an account in less than a minute, *as long as it's been posted there before.*</u> What this means is:

If you've already been keeping your books in the QuickBooks file you are currently working on BEFORE picking up this book, *you will actually have to do less work.* Most vendors and customers will already be entered and have transactions posted to the appropriate expense accounts. If you haven't, this means a few extra steps where you will assign vendors to specific expense accounts, but it will still be fairly quick and easy. I'll try to slow down as much as I can, but these things are going to happen really fast with or without me.

Also, keep in mind that CHECKS WILL NOT BE ENTERED IN THIS STEP. The bank does not detail ANY information about checks except for the check number and check amount. That means YOU WILL HAVE TO ENTER ALL CHECKS MANUALLY. Yes it sucks... BUT, if you were to use mostly your credit or debit card from today on, you can save all of that bookkeeping data entry time when you do these steps again next year (or when your bookkeeper has to do their regular day-to-day data entry).

So... having said that... here we go:

1. Open your online banking screen by going to **"Banking,"** **"Online Banking," "Online Banking Center."**

   - You can also click the "Online Banking" icon in your toolbar, if you see it there. It looks like this:

The newer versions of QuickBooks will pop up a screen that looks something like this:

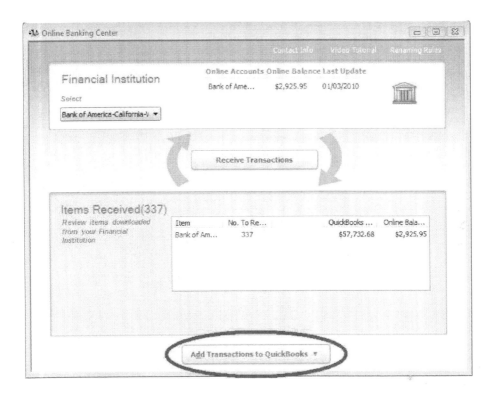

Click the **"Add Transactions to QuickBooks"** button (shown above).

Older versions of QuickBooks will look like this:

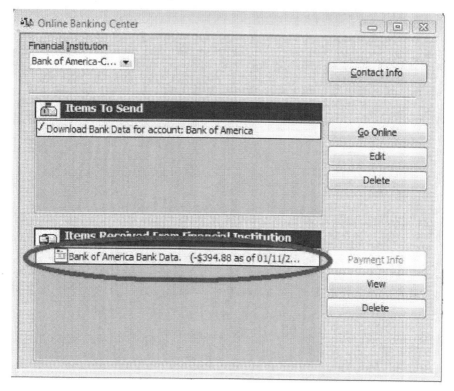

Double click the bottom yellow-ish bar (circled above).

2. Once you've double-clicked the corresponding button, you will be taken to a "Match Transactions" screen where we will **"Add Multiple"** transactions. (Click the corresponding buttons in your version of QuickBooks.)

~ 41 ~

## Newer Versions of QuickBooks will look like this:

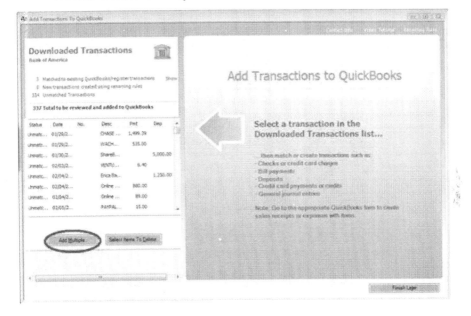

Older Versions of QuickBooks will look like this:

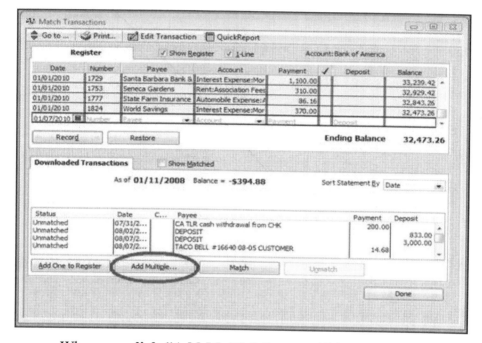

When you **click "Add Multiple"**, you will be taken to a screen that will show you all transactions that CAN be posted automatically. (These matches will be based on previous entries.) When you **click "Add Selected" or "Record"**, all of those transactions will automatically be entered and posted with no further work needed from you. This will take approximately five minutes.

3. Once all of the "Multiple Items" are gone from the "Add Multiple Transaction list", you are then going to **"Add One**

**Transaction to the Register"**. This step will be more time consuming than the last step, but can still go pretty quickly.

    a.  In older versions, you will need to go back to the "Match Transactions" screen and **select a transaction from the "Downloaded Transactions" register** on the bottom (as shown in red below):

Once an item is selected, you will **click the "Add One to Register" button** where you will most be likely be taken to a "Name Not Found" screen. From there, **select "Create Alias", type in the name of the Vendor/Customer and Press "OK" or "Quick Add."** You will be taken back to the "Match Transactions" screen, and in the Upper "Register" your transaction will be the last entry (as shown in yellow above). **In the upper "Register", fill in the "Account" name with the type of Expense, and then click "Record."**

b. In newer versions, you are going to remain in the "Add Multiple Transactions" screen, which looks like this:

To post ONE entry, simply **check the transaction box
to the left and fill in the Payee square with the
Vendor/Customer Name and the Account Square
with the Type of Expense**, as shown above. Then **click
"Add Selected."**

4. Once you've added ONE entry from ONE company, **click on
"Add Multiple" again** and QuickBooks will find and list all the
other entries with the same Company/Transaction ID of the item
that you just posted. It will then give you a list of all matching

~ 46 ~

transactions that can be posted to the same expense account – just as you did in Step 3.

5.  **Repeat Steps 3 through 5 until all entries are gone.**

*(Important Note:* <u>**When entering Credit Card Payments from your Checking Account,**</u> *you are going to enter the* <u>**Name of the Credit Card**</u> *in the Expense Field. Do NOT expense it to any other categories as this will create a double entry problem for you to deal with later on.)*

- <u>*To do this even faster,*</u> *enter several single entries for different companies* **before** *hitting "Add Multiple." Then QuickBooks will find all those companies and categorize them faster than if you were to do them one at a time.*

**STEP 3: IF AND ONLY IF your credit card does NOT offer the free Business Expense report at the end of the year,** repeat the steps listed in STEP 2 for all of your downloadable Credit Card files. If your bank DOES offer the Business Expense Report, skip this step and move onto **STEP 4**.

## *NOW FOR THE SUCKY STUFF - MANUAL DATA ENTRY*

That's right – I said it: This is the part that sucks. Really Sucks. I mean – make-you-cry-to-your-mama *sucks*. It's time for Manual Data Entry, and there's no way around it. Believe me, if there were, I would have already found it.

If you're not shuddering in horror at the image this brings to mind (that of you bent over your keyboard for the next several hours), then that's probably for the best. You really don't want to think too much about it or you might start ripping your hair out. (I know this is the part where I usually get weepy.)

At this point, you've had QuickBooks do as much as it possibly can on its own, so you have to do the rest. This means, we're going to enter everything NOT in your downloaded transactions. These transactions include All Transactions BEFORE the date your bank allowed you to download your Web Connect / IIF File – including deposits, electronic POS payments, and ALL checks. But take heart – there are still plenty of shortcuts we're going to use.

So hurry! Grab an Espresso and come back. You're going to need it!

Ready? Ok.

## STEP 4: Enter the Highlighted Transactions on Your Bank Statements and "Memorize" Them (Using the Ctrl + M Button)

Remember how you highlighted transactions that repeat month after month in CHAPTER 1 – Item 5? The reason we did that is two-fold: 1) the highlighting makes finding those transactions and entering them in this step easier and faster; and 2) the highlighting will keep you from double-entering those same transactions later in this process.

Having said that, we are now going to take those transactions, enter them, and then "Memorize" them. The Good News is: YOU ONLY HAVE TO DO THIS ONCE, and it's easy to do.

Memorizing a Transaction involves Entering the Transaction as you would normally, BUT **Pressing _Ctrl_ + _M_** <u>BEFORE</u> you **"Save and Close"** it. (Details to enter individual transactions are in STEPS 5 TO 10 below, in case you need directions on how to enter checks, deposits, credit cards, etc.)

## <u>Quick Step-By-Step Memorizing Involves:</u>

1. **Press *Ctrl + M*.**
2. In the screen that pops up, choose "Enter Automatically", and then the frequency (weekly, monthly, quarterly, etc.).
3. Choose the next date you want the transaction entered (which is going to be the transaction for the NEXT month – Thus, you would choose February if you are entering January's transaction).
4. Choose the number of transactions remaining (which is useful for items such as car payments), and the number of days to enter the transaction in advance if you're going to mail that transaction in the future.
5. **Click "OK"** to return to the Original Transaction.
6. **Press *Ctrl + Enter*** to Save That Transaction for THAT MONTH.
7. **Repeat** with the next highlighted transaction.
8. When you're done with that first transaction, you're done with this step and are ready for STEP 5.

(Go to www.OneHourBookkeeper.com/AYWBonsues for a printable version of these shortcuts.)

*Important Note*: <u>Once the transaction is Memorized, you can simply</u> <u>Close and then Reopen QuickBooks and QuickBooks will automatically</u> <u>enter ALL of those transaction from the first entry up to TODAY.</u> *That means, if you're working on the 2007 books for your business, these transactions will repeat all the way up to 2010 (if you're entering in 2010).*

## STEP 5:  Enter All Checks

Checks are the one thing that cannot be matched by QuickBooks, so you will have to enter every single one of them manually.  The fastest way to do this is to use your check register, if you have one.  If you don't have one, then you are going to use the checks you put in sequential order.  But take heart – QuickBooks will automatically recall previous transactions and auto-fill many of the fields.  Once you get into a rhythm, this can go pretty quickly.

*For now, you are going to skip all transactions done with your debit card or with bill pay.  We are going to stick solely to checks with check numbers in the interest of going fast.*

Now, pull out that check register and your checks and let's begin with January.

(In hopes of making the steps easier, I've color-coded them in Rainbow Colors on the "Check" below.)

1. To "Write Checks," you are going to **Press *Ctrl* + *W***. This will open up a screen that looks like a check and a register (see below).

(Go to www.OneHourBookkeeper.com/AYWBonsues for a printable COLOR version of all of the following tables.)

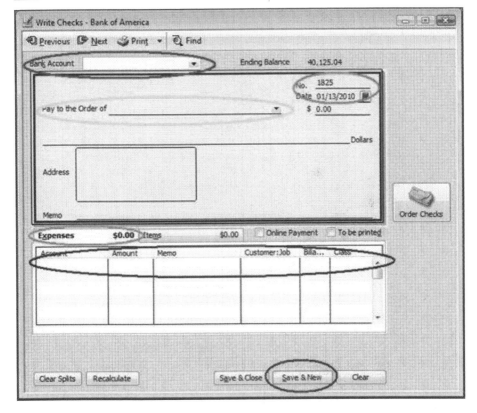

By E.T. Barton       &       Robin E. Davis

2.  Next, **enter the Bank Account Name into the Bank Field** (if it is not already pre-filled due to what you would have set in your Preferences). This step is shown in the check above in red. You will only have to do this step once since the next time you open a check, the bank name will be automatically filled in. **Press Tab** to move to the next field.

3.  **Enter the Check Number** in the Number Field (as shown in orange). The next time you pull up a check, this number will be automatically filled in with the next check number in sequential order , which means you can skip this step next time (except when there's a missing check). **Press Tab** to move to the next field.

4.  **Enter the Date of the Check** (also shown in orange).

    a.  There are two ways you can enter the date quickly. One is to type the numbers without the " / " in the middle. For example, to enter a transaction on January 15th, 2009, you could type 011509 instead of 01/15/09. It may seem like it won't save much time, but it actually can.

    b.  The other way is to *change your computer's date to the year of data entry*. If you change the date of your computer to any day in 2009, you can skip many key

~ 53 ~

strokes because QuickBooks will think you are IN 2009. So, for the date above, you could enter 0115 instead of 01/15/09 or 01/15 and QuickBooks will automatically format the year for you.

6. **Press Tab** to move to the Payee field (shown in yellow).

7. **Type the Name of the Person / Company** that received and cashed the check. As you type, the name will auto fill in based on the vendors you have already paid. The more letters you type, the more names will disappear from the drop down list. Then, you can either use the arrow keys to move up and down the Vendor list, or keep typing until only the name you need shows.

   - At this point, if everything is pre-filled, you can hit Ctrl + Enter to Save this Transaction and Create a new one—because you're done with this check. If the Expense Field is not filled in, go ahead and continue.

8. **Press Tab** and you will be moved to the next field – which should be the Expense Account field.

9. Before you enter the type of expense, make sure that the "Expenses" Tab is selected (as shown in green above). If you are in the Items tab, your bookkeeping can get all screwed up.

This is a one-time change and once done, it will automatically be on the "Expenses" tab every time until you choose the other tab.

10. Now that you are in the Expenses "Account" field (as shown in blue), one of two things will happen.

   a. If you have entered that vendor before, the "Account" Field and "Amount" Field will automatically be filled in. **If the check is expensed correctly, simply Click *Ctrl + Enter*** to save the check and move onto the next check. (This would be the same as pressing the "Save & New" button in purple.) ⟨OBJ⟩

   b. If you haven't entered that vendor before, **choose the Expense Type**. This is a drop-down field, so you can either search for it if you're new to entering checks, or you can type the name of the expense and QuickBooks will auto-fill it just as it did in the Payee Field. **Press *Ctrl + Enter*,** which is the same thing as clicking "Save and New".

11. **Repeat all of these steps until all the checks are entered.**

---

**Write Your Checks & Debits**

*Ctrl + W*

**(All Versions)**

1. Enter the Bank Account Name into the Bank Field – *Tab*

2. Enter the Check Number – *Tab*

3. Enter the Date – *Tab*

4. Type the Name of the Person / Company in the Payee Field – *Tab*

5. *(If the transaction is not expensed correctly, tab down to the Expense Field and enter the type of expense.)*

6. Press *Ctrl + Enter* (or "Save & New")

7. Repeat Each Step until All Checks are Entered.

(Go to www.OneHourBookkeeper.com/AYWBonsues for a printable version of these shortcuts.)

---

~ 56 ~

## STEP 6: Get Out Your Bank Statements, and Enter All Debits From Your Debit Card Or Bill Pay.


**BUT REMEMBER... You are entering ALL transactions EXCEPT the transactions downloaded from your bank AND ALL the transactions you highlighted on the bank statements.** This means you're going to start in January and stop when you get to whatever was the earliest date your bank let you download.

All of these transaction types will be listed on your bank statements. Simply start with January and **Repeat all of the steps you just did in STEP 5.** The biggest change, however, is how you are going to "Number" these transactions differently than you did when you entered the checks. Instead of continuing on with the check numbers from earlier, you are going to change the number to something completely different. *What I like to do is put EFT or EP in front of the number so that I know by sight that it's an Electronic Funds Transfer or an Electronic Payment.* A good example of this would be to make your very first debit card / bill pay transaction in January to be "numbered" as EFT1. Then, the next check you open will automatically fill itself in as EFT2. This will help you know how many times you use your debit card or bill pay in a year.

Go as quickly as you can through this step.

## STEP 7: <u>Manually</u> Enter Any Credit Card Summary Expense Reports

The fastest and easiest way to enter all of your credit card expenses for the year is just to enter the summary information. If you prefer to enter all of the transactions individually by date and month, feel free – the step-by-step instructions are listed under STEP 8. If you prefer to save time, however, then do the following:

1. **Click "Banking", then "Enter Credit Card Charges."** You should see an "Enter Credit Card Charges" screen that looks something like the picture below. (Again, I've highlighted the different entries in Rainbow Colors to make data entry easier.)

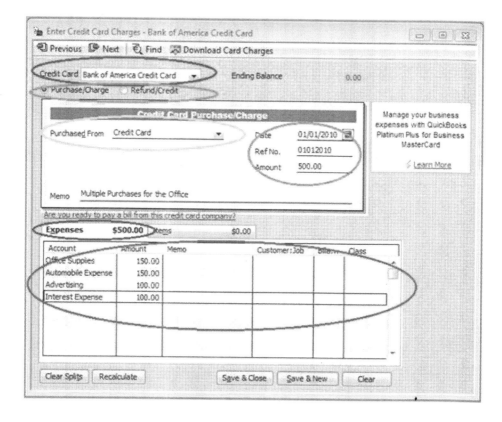

2. Next, **Enter the Credit Card Name into the Credit Card Field** (as shown in red). **Press Tab** to move to the next field.

3. **Make sure that "Purchase / Charge" is highlighted** (as shown in orange). **Press Tab Twice** to move to the "Purchased From" field.

4. **Enter the Date as 12/31 of the year you are entering** (shown in green). Since we are entering the summary expense for the

By E.T. Barton     &     Robin E. Davis

whole year only once, the last day of the year will make this easier to find if you ever need. **Press Tab** to move to the next field.

5. **Enter the Reference Number** in the Reference Number Field (also shown in green). I would use something like "SR1" for the first transaction from the Summary Report. **Press Tab** to move to the next field.

6. **Enter the Amount of the Expense you are entering** (in green). For example, if you are entering the "Office Supply" expense, then just enter that amount. The other amounts will be entered when you repeat each of these steps. **Press Tab Twice** to get to the Expense Account field.

7. Just like with the checks, you need to make sure that the "Expenses" Tab is selected (as shown in blue above).

8. Also, just like when you entered checks, one of two things will happen:

    a. If you have entered that vendor before, the "Account" Field and "Amount" Field will automatically be filled in. **If the check is expensed correctly, simply Click *Ctrl + Enter* to** enter the next Summary Expense Amount.

b.   If you haven't entered that vendor before, **choose the Expense Type**, then **Press *Ctrl* + *Enter*,** to "Save and (Create a) New" credit card transaction.

- *Quick Note:   One fast way to enter credit card charges is to enter all charges by STATEMENT as a single credit card entry.   For example, the picture above is for a credit card statement entered as a single entry on January 1ˢᵗ, 2010.   As you can see, the expenses from that month are categorized in purple.   By doing this, you can enter 12 single monthly entries instead of multiple daily entries, and thus save time.   Then, you could Reconcile your Credit Card Account 3 months at a time (Quarterly) instead of monthly and still provide a more accurate Quarterly P&L for prior year comparisons to future years.*

9.   **Repeat all of these steps** until all the Credit Card Expenses are entered from the Summary Report.

10. **Repeat with the next Credit Card Business Summary.**

## Write Your Checks & Debits
### *"Banking – Enter Credit Card Charges"*
### (All Versions)

1. Enter the Credit Card Name into the Credit Card Field – *Tab* (3 times)

2. Enter the Payee Name – *Tab*

3. Enter the Date – *Tab*

4. Enter the Reference Number – *Tab*

5. Enter the Amount – *Tab*

6. *(If the transaction is not expensed correctly, tab down to the Expense Field and enter the type of expense.)*

7. Press *Ctrl + Enter* (Save & New)

8. Repeat Each Step until All Credit Card Transactions are Entered.

(Go to www.OneHourBookkeeper.com/AYWBonsues for a printable version of these shortcuts.)

## STEP 8: If You Do Not Have a Credit Card Summary Expense Report, Manually Enter ALL Credit Card Transactions by Date.

You ONLY need to do this step if you were UNABLE to download your credit card transactions from STEP 2. If that is the case, you must manually enter all credit card transactions by hand. The steps to do this are exactly the same as those detailed out in STEP 7 – so follow those steps to enter each transaction individually. *(Obviously, this could take as much data entry time as it took to enter your checks.)*

- When entering Credit Card refunds, you will select "Refund / Credit" in STEP 7-C in lieu of "Purchase / Charge."

- When entering payments – DON'T! Payments should have already been entered when you entered either your bank account transactions, or your checks.

- AGAIN, you can enter one single transaction to cover all the expenses of the month if you really wish to save time.

## STEP 9: Enter the Daily Sales from either your Cash Register Tapes or from Individual Receipts.

When entering Sales, there are three ways that you will want to go about it. 1) You can enter daily sales totals, *which means 365 separate entries;* 2) You can enter monthly sales, which means *12 separate entries* (give or take); or 3) You can post all Sales deposits as "Sales" from the bank statement. When making this decision, there are two questions you need to answer:

1. *What do I plan to do with the entries?*
    a. I want to use the entries to analyze which days are my top sales days in a given year, and which products are my best sellers. I will then use those sales as a benchmark with which to compare future sales.
    b. I want to use the entries to analyze which months are my top sales months.
    c. I just want the information for my taxes.

If your answer is Choice a, then you're going to enter 365 individual entries. If b or c, then you will be doing roughly 12 to 100 entries (give or take), depending upon the number of times you physically went to the bank to make a deposit. For example, if you only made a deposit once a week, you will only have 52 entries.

And the second question you will need to answer is:

2. *How much detail do I really want or need?*
   a. I want as much detail as possible because I plan to use this to analyze my business's growth, best-selling products and high-sales days.
   b. I'm not so keen on detail. Again, I just want this for my taxes.

If you answer is Choice a, then you'll want to gather the register tapes or sales receipts for the past year. (Register Tapes will be faster since they will already have the summed-up totals for each of the 365 days. If you are using sales receipts, then you will want to use the totals you added up in CHAPTER 1.)

If your answer is b, then all you'll need is your bank statements.

So, go ahead and pull out either your daily sales receipts or your bank statements, and let's get started.

*Quick Note: If you are trying to get the books ready for tax time, you might want to begin tracking sales in the Current Year rather in lieu of recreating them in a Previous Year.*

1. **Go to "Banking" – "Make Deposits"** to open the "Make Deposits" Screen, which should look something like this:

2. In the "Deposit To" box, **Enter the Name of the Checking Account** where you deposited your sales (as shown in red). **Press *Tab*.**

~ 66 ~

3. In the "Date" box (shown in orange), **Enter the date of the first deposit** on your Bank Statement. **Press *Tab* twice** to get to the "Received From" box (circled in yellow).

4. In the "Received From" box, **Enter the name "Customers"** for now. (Most likely, you will have to add this if you haven't before. A "Name Not Found" Screen will pop up and you can **Select "Quick Add"** to quickly add "Customers" to the Customers Category.) **Press *Tab*.**

5. In the "From Account" box, you are going to enter the Category of "Sales".

   - If you have not entered "Sales" as a category before, you will be given a chance to "Set it Up" now. In the "Add New Account: Choose Account Type" box, **Select "Income" and "Continue."** In the "Add New Account" box, leave all the information as-is, BUT under "Tax-Line Mapping", **Select "Schedule C: Gross Receipts or Sales."** Then, **Press *Ctrl* + *Enter* (or "Save & Close").**

6. Tab to the "Amount" box, and **Enter the Amount of the Deposit.**

7. **Press *Ctrl* + *Enter* or "Save & New"** (shown in green) to save the deposit and create a second one.

8. Repeat these steps until all deposits from all Bank Statements have been entered.

## STEP 10: Enter Merchant Account Sales Information by Month:

1. Take your Merchant Account Statements and find the "Total Amount Deposited for the Month." Enter that number as Sales under the corresponding Account Name Register in the same way that you did in STEP 8.

2. Then, find the "Total Refunded Amount for the Month" and Enter those transactions as a Check under the corresponding Account Name Register.

# CHAPTER 3:

# Your Day's Work is Done!

# Now It's Time to Double Check Your Work

# ...Or Not!

Now I'm going to say something of which most accountants or bookkeepers would not approve: IF YOU'VE COMPLETED EVERY STEP IN CHAPTER 2, YOU COULD STOP RIGHT HERE IF YOU WANT. I won't be mad. Fact is, if you reached this step, you've PROBABLY entered every expense and income transaction you could possibly add. From a practical standpoint, you could print out your reports and take them to an accountant or tax professional and they will be able to do your taxes.

HOWEVER, if you want to be ABSOLUTELY CERTAIN that you claimed every expense you could possibly claim, then you're going to want to double check your work. As difficult as this sounds, it's actually *really easy.* All you have to do are bank / credit card reconciliations. Each reconciliation could take as little as 3 minutes per month per account – or as long as 30 minutes per account per month – depending on how accurately you entered everything before this.

In other words, if you want to double check your work by doing a reconciliation, expect to spend about another 30 minutes to 1 hour per account to be reconciled. Keep in mind, THIS DOES NOT INCLUDE CREDIT CARDS WHERE YOU ENTERED A BUSINESS EXPENSE REPORT! (Woo hoo, right?) This only is necessary for accounts where you had to do a LOT of manual data entry.

Having said that... Do you want to continue on?

**Do you?**

Well, okay... if you're in; I'm in.

Get out your Bank Statements again. You're gonna need 'em.

**BUT REMEMBER: If you haven't already, <u>Close and Open QuickBooks ONCE so that ALL of your Memorized Transactions will enter automatically</u>. If you do not or have not, you WILL find those transactions missing when you go to reconcile.**

*Another Quick Note: Doing QUARTERLY reconciliations – especially for the credit card statements – is a quicker and easier option than monthly reconciliations. However, it can be a little more challenging for bank accounts, depending upon the number of entries per month you entered. So, my recommendation is do quarterly reconciliations for everything but the bank account.*

## STEP 11: Begin Bank Reconciliations

As I said before, if you missed a lot of things when you did your manual bank entry, finding and fixing those things could expand your work an extra hour. For now, we're going to assume you've entered everything correctly, and we will jump right into the reconciliation.

To reconcile, you will do the following:

1. Go to **"Banking"** – **"Reconcile"**

- For all versions, the screen is pretty much going to look like this:

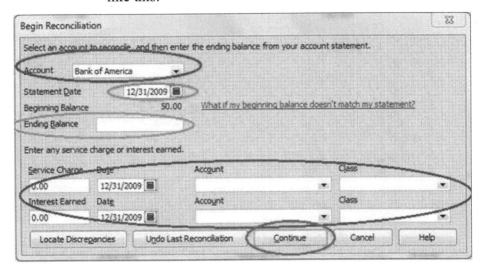

Again, this is Rainbow-Color Coded for ease of understanding.

2. Once you see this screen, you are going to **Fill-In the Name of the Account** that you are reconciling in the Account Field (as shown in red). Press **_Tab_**.

3. In the Date Field, you are going to **Enter the ENDING Statement Date from your Bank Account Statement** (as shown in Orange). Press **_Tab_**.

~ 72 ~

4. If you have NEVER done a bank reconciliation before, AND you have transactions that need to be reconciled from the year before, you can either:

- Do all of the steps listed here for previous bank statements to get the most accurate bank balance possible (which is only necessary if you are keeping your books as detailed as you can), OR

- You can reconcile all transactions as of 12/31/THAT-YEAR (NOT the year you are working on) and QuickBooks will make an adjusting entry for you as of 12/31/THAT-YEAR. <u>This step is my recommendation for those who are interested in saving the most time.</u>

  i. To do this step, make the ending date "12/31/THAT-YEAR" and continue.

5. You will have skipped over the Beginning Balance line (shown in yellow), which you can NOT fill in. If this is the first time you've ever reconciled the account, you may see a $0.00 balance here. If that's the case, ignore it for now... you will be making an adjusting entry later in this step.

6. You should now be in the Ending Balance Field (circled in green above). **Enter the Ending Bank Balance from the Bank Statement** in the square and **Press *Tab***.

~ 73 ~

- (If you are reconciling for the year before, you are going to put in the BEGINNING Bank Balance from the Bank Statement as your Ending Bank Balance.)

7. If you have Bank Service Charges or Interest Earned, you are going to enter those amounts and accounts in the appropriate boxes (shown in blue above).

8. **Press *Ctrl + Enter* (or "Continue"** – shown in purple) to move to the next "Reconcile" Screen, which will look like this:

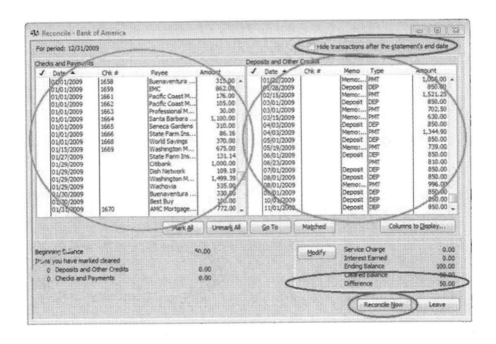

Again, this is color-coded for easier understanding.

9. In the Reconcile Screen, you will notice a little box in the upper right hand corner that says "Hide Transactions After the Statement's End Date." (See red in the picture above.) It is my recommendation that you **Check That Box** so that you will only have to work with items that would have cleared in the time frame we are reconciling for. If you do not do that, you will have to search through hundreds of transactions manually to find the ones you need, and this can increase your likelihood of missing things. So, for now, go ahead and check that box and see 11/12ths of your work magically disappear. (Don't worry, it's not really gone – it's just hidden.)

10. On the right hand side of the screen, you will see all "Deposits and Other Credits" (as shown in orange). Here, you are going to compare this list to your Bank Statement and **Select All the Deposits that Cleared** during that Bank Statement Reconciliation Period. (I'm having you do this side first because it's easier and faster than the "Checks and Payments" side.) **Make sure the <u>amounts</u> also are the same, because if they are not, you can spend hours trying to figure out why your balance is off by dollars or even pennies.**

   - This step can be VERY complicated if you don't do it right. To keep it simple, when you Select a Transaction in the Reconciliation box in QuickBooks, BE SURE TO PUT A CHECKMARK next to the matching AMOUNT on your bank statement in pen / pencil. Anything that IS on the Bank Statement, but is NOT in the QuickBooks file, UNDERLINE it on the Bank Statement. <u>You will either "Find" or Re-Enter the underlined/missing transactions later</u> (like this):

- If any amounts are off, double click on that transaction in THIS screen and that transaction will open. (If it doesn't open, triple click it so that QuickBooks won't think you are just selecting the item for clearing.)

- If you are doing a reconciliation for the year before, make sure to check off all items BEFORE the transaction date, but BE VERY CAREFUL that you don't select checks that might clear in a month or two. It's a bit tricky, but you'll figure it out as you go along. And when in doubt, skip it.

11. Now double check that you've gotten all of your deposits in correctly. To do this, simply compare the "Items that you have marked or cleared – Deposits or Other Credits" line (as shown in yellow) to the "Deposit" amount on your Bank Statement. If you entered everything correctly, then these two numbers should

be identical. <u>If your totals are not the same, then you will need to "Find" and Fix the transaction, or Re-Enter it altogether.</u> Here's how they should match up if they're cleared:

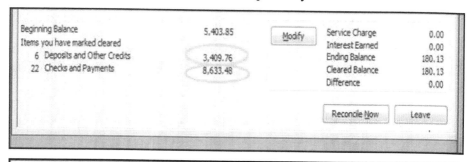

12. Okay...assuming that your Cleared Balance in QuickBooks matches your Deposit Balance on your Bank Statement, you are now going to do the exact same thing you did in Step 10 for the "Checks and Payments" side (as shown in green from the original bank reconciliation screen).

- *Note: "Check Numbers" will be listed in Numerical order and be near the TOP of your list of transactions. Anything with Letters AND Numbers will be listed numerically after that. Any transactions WITHOUT numbers (and yes, there will be some), will either be near the top or the bottom of your list depending on your version of QuickBooks. So, make sure to check your list thoroughly from top to bottom when you are searching for transactions. <u>If any transactions are missing, "Find" them as you did before and Fix them or Re-Enter them.</u>*

- Again, put checkmarks and underlines on the Bank Statement as you select transactions in QuickBooks, and double check the numbers as you go in order to avoid any easy-to-miss discrepancies.

13. Once you've gone through the entire bank statement, and you've done a "Ctrl + Find" for the missing transactions, go ahead and re-enter those underlined transactions on the Bank Statement as you did in CHAPTER 2. Then, go back to the reconciliation screen, find those items this time, and make sure to put checkmarks next to them.

14. At this point, the "Difference" line (shown in blue) should be $0.00. Once the "Difference" is $0.00, then you know you have accurately cleared the account. If that is NOT the case, and everything is fixed or entered, then:

- Check to make sure everything is checked that should be checked and that nothing got "un-checked" as you went along (because believe me, accidentally un-checking things is super-easy to do in QuickBooks).

- If everything IS checked, you need to make an adjusting entry by creating a CHECK or DEPOSIT with the <u>Amount of the Difference AND a Date of "12/31/THE-YEAR-BEFORE"</u>. By doing so, you will be able to find this adjustment if & when you find the missing information or errors at a later date.

- *Just a Thought: It is also a good idea to use these steps to Reconcile the bank account for the LAST MONTH OF THE YEAR BEFORE – the sole purpose being to get the correct BEGINNING BALANCE of the checking account. To do this, you would make a deposit to open the account (probably in the same amount of the "Difference" from the yellow section), then clear that deposit and reconcile your account for "12/31/YEAR-*

*BEFORE" so that your Ending Balance will become the Beginning Balance you need for YOUR-YEAR-OF-DATA-ENTRY.*

15. When you are finished, **Press *Ctrl* + *Enter* (or "Reconcile Now"** – circled in blue on the Reconcile screen) to finish up the reconciliation.

16. You will be prompted to "Print the Reconciliation." Whether or not you do so is entirely up to you and whether you want a printed transaction or not.

    - *If it was my company and I had a bookkeeper, I WOULD want this printed manually because it is too easy to change or delete a report from QuickBooks later on and a printed report cannot be changed – only burned or destroyed. If I were doing the data entry and the reconciliations myself, I would simply save a PDF'd copy on my computer.*

17. Now **Repeat** all of these steps for every month or quarter that follows.

18. Once you've finished December, do this for all other bank accounts and credit card accounts.

19. You can also do this for Merchant Accounts, if you want to be absolutely thorough, although _we DON'T recommend it because this is WAY too much work_!

And that's EVERYTHING. You should now be completely finished and ready for your accountant.

# CHAPTER 4:

# Getting Your Reports Ready

# For Your Accountant or Tax Man

Can you believe your day is done?

Now, it's tax time. You can either get a list of reports your accountant / tax man wants from you for your business and personal taxes, or you can give them a special "Accountant's Backup" that they can upload into *their* QuickBooks file and get the reports they need. Obviously, giving them an Accountant's Copy will be easier for you than printing out all the reports, but if you're going to a Tax Man, it's less likely they will have QuickBooks and more likely they will want printed reports. Read on for more step-by-step instructions (and take heart – we're almost done).

## *ACCOUNTANT'S BACKUP*

*Quick Note: If you are having an accountant double check your work, they can modify their version of the Accountant's Copy which you can then upload into your version. For NEWER versions, you will be able to select a "Dividing Date" that limits when you can and cannot change transactions and when your Accountant can and cannot change transactions.*

To get the Accountant's Copy:

1. Go to **"File", "Accountant's Copy", and then "Save File"** (for newer QuickBooks versions).
2. **Choose "Accountant's Copy" or "Portable or Backup File."** Then **Click "Next."**
3. For Newer Versions, **Choose your "Dividing Date"** then **"Okay"** when prompted.

4. You will then be prompted to save your file somewhere. And that's it. The file is now ready to be copied to a disc or emailed to your accountant.

## *PRINTING REPORTS*

This is also easy. To print any reports you need:

1. **Go to "Reports."**
2. Go to "Accountant & Taxes" or "Company & Financial." What you print out will depend on the list your Accountant / Tax Man wants tells you to print out.
3. From the report, you can customize the date and different filters, and you can also email or print those reports. I would click "Email" in the toolbar of the report, and then enter the corresponding email address.

And that's it. You are officially done.

Did it take you one day, or did it take you longer? I would really like to know. Email E.T. at ETBarton@OneHourBookkeeper.com with any comments, questions or problems and we'll do what we can to help.

# *APPENDICES*

## *Shortcuts that are the same in QuickBooks as they are in Excel and Word:*

- *Tab* = Moves to the Next Data Entry Field
- *Shift* + *Tab* = Moves to the Previous Data Entry Field
- *Ctrl* + *Tab* = Moves to the next open window within the program
- *Ctrl* + *F* = <u>F</u>ind
- (In QuickBooks, this shortcut will open a Find Box that will help you find transactions and mistakes.)
- *Ctrl* + *C* = <u>C</u>opy
- *Ctrl* + *V* = Paste
- *Ctrl* + *P* = <u>P</u>rint

## *QuickBooks Shortcuts:*

- *Ctrl* + *Enter* = "Save and New" / "Next" or "Okay" (depending on the screen you're in; basically, *this is going to be your new best friend*, and the most used shortcut you can use).
- *Ctrl* + *W* = <u>W</u>rite Checks (This will be your *second* most used shortcut since you're about to do a lot of "check writing.")
- *Ctrl* + *R* = <u>R</u>egister (This will go to your default check register first, but you can also use it to select a register for ANYthing... customers, vendors, accounts, items, etc. This will be your *third* most used key.)

- *Ctrl + D* = **D**elete  (If you're not familiar with QuickBooks, this shortcut may actually become your most used shortcut.  This will delete anything you currently have open—check, invoice, sales receipt, etc.)

- *Ctrl + M* = **M**emorize (When you are in a transaction that you know is going to repeat itself monthly, weekly, bi-monthly, etc., then you're going to want to memorize the transaction.  This way, QuickBooks will enter it automatically for you multiple times, thus saving you time.)

- *Ctrl + H* = **H**istory (This shortcut will help you find "Linked" Transactions.  For example, if you are in a deposit and want to see if that deposit is "Linked" to a customer payment, you would use this shortcut to see the History associated with that transaction.)

(Go to  www.OneHourBookkeeper.com/AYWBonsues  for a printable version of these shortcuts.)

## Post Your Bank Transactions From the "Add Transactions to QuickBooks" Screen (<u>Newer Versions</u>)

1. Click "Add Multiple"

2. Check the Transaction Box

3. Fill in the Payee square with the Vendor/Customer Name - *Tab*

4. Fill in the Account Square with the Type of Expense

5. *Ctrl + Enter* (or "Add Selected")

6. Repeat Each Step Until All Transactions are Gone.

# Post Your Bank Transactions From the "Add Transactions to QuickBooks" Screen (Older Versions)

1. Click "Add Multiple"
2. "Add One Transaction to the Register"
3. Select one transaction from the "Downloaded Transactions" register
4. Click the "Add One to Register" button
5. *(If it's a new vendor: Select "Create Alias", type in the name of the Vendor/Customer and Press "OK" or "Quick Add")*
6. In the upper "Register", fill in the "Account" name with the type of Expense
7. *Ctrl + Enter* (or "Record")
8. Repeat Each Step Until All Transactions are Gone.

## Write Your Checks & Debits
### *"Banking – Enter Credit Card Charges"*
### <u>(All Versions)</u>

1. Enter the Credit Card Name into the Credit Card Field – *Tab* (<u>3 times</u>)

2. Enter the Payee Name – *Tab*

3. Enter the Date – *Tab*

4. Enter the Reference Number – *Tab*

5. Enter the Amount – *Tab*

6. *(If the transaction is not expensed correctly, tab down to the Expense Field and enter the type of expense.)*

7. Press *Ctrl + Enter* (Save & New)

8. Repeat Each Step until All Credit Card Transactions are Entered.

# Quick-Step Checklist:

1. _____ QuickBooks Downloaded and Your Company Information Already Set Up

2. _____ Make Sure You Have Online Access to Your Bank Accounts and Credit Card Accounts.

3. _____ Check with Your Bank to See if Your Bank Account Information Can Be Downloaded.

4. _____ Get All Your Bank Statements and Put Them in Sequential Order by Month.

5. _____ Highlight All Repetitive Transactions on Your Bank Statements

6. _____ Get a Credit Card Business Expense Report, if Available. If it is NOT Available, Organize All Credit Card Statements in Sequential Order by Month.

7. _____ Get Your Check Register, if You Kept One.

8. _____ Organize All Hardcopies of Checks into Sequential Order.

9. _____ If You Accept Credit Cards for Payment (and Can't Download a Full Year's Worth of Transactions), You Will Need Your Monthly Merchant Account Statements.

10. _____ Tally Up Your Sales

11. _____ Change Your QuickBooks Preferences to Save Time

12. _____ Setup QuickBooks to Access Your Online Accounts

# To "Find" Any Transaction in QuickBooks

- "Find" the transaction by Pressing **Ctrl + F**. This will open the Find screen, which looks like this (in all versions of QuickBooks):

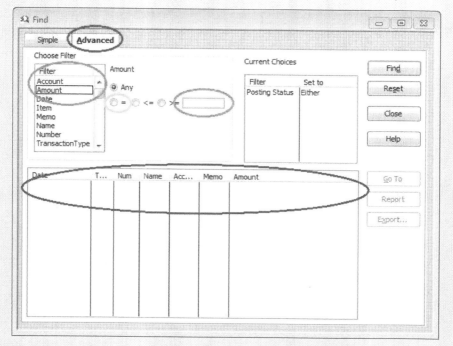

- **Click on the Advanced Tab** at the top (shown in red).
- **Select "Amount"** in the "Filter" box (shown in orange).
- **Click on the "=" sign** in the Amount Area (shown in yellow).
- **Enter the Amount** in the box (shown in green).
- Press **Ctrl + Enter (or "Find")**.

~ 93 ~

- All Matching Transactions will show up in the bottom (as shown in blue).
- If you see your transaction, **double click it to open it**.
- Check to make sure all the information is correct and change anything that is not. Press *Ctrl + Enter* to save the transaction.

# **Quick-Step Nitty Gritty Checklist:**

_____ STEP 1: Upload your Bank's Web Connect File into QuickBooks

_____ STEP 2: Post Your "Web Connect" / "IIF" Files to the Appropriate Accounts.

_____ STEP 3: <u>IF AND ONLY IF your credit card does NOT offer the free Business Expense report at the end of the year</u>, repeat the steps listed in STEP 2 for all of your downloadable Credit Card files.

_____ STEP 4: Enter the Highlighted Transactions on Your Bank Statements and "Memorize" Them (Using the Ctrl + M Button)

_____ STEP 5: Enter All Checks

_____ STEP 6: Get Out Your Bank Statements, and Enter All Debits From Your Debit Card Or Bill Pay.

_____ STEP 7: <u>Manually</u> Enter Any Credit Card Summary Expense Reports

_____ STEP 8: IF YOU DO NOT HAVE A CREDIT CARD

SUMMARY EXPENSE REPORT, <u>Manually</u> Enter ALL Credit Card Transactions by Date.

_____ STEP 9:  Enter the Daily Sales from either your Cash Register Tapes or from Individual Receipts.

_____ STEP 10:  Enter Merchant Account Sales Information by Month

_____ STEP 11:  Begin Bank Reconciliations

## So What Did You Think?

We'd love to get your opinion.
Please email E.T. Barton at
ETBarton@OneHourBookkeeper.com

**Also, if you would like to help us promote this book and pass it on to other small business owners,**
## please leave a review at Amazon.

---

## Other One Hour Bookkeeper Products:

THE ONE HOUR BOOKKEEPING METHOD:
How To Do Your Books In One Hour Or Less

HOW TO START A LUCRATIVE
VIRTUAL BOOKKEEPING BUSINESS:
A Step-by-Step Guide to Working Less and Making More
in the Bookkeeping Industry

10 WAYS TO SAVE MONEY ON
BOOKKEEPING & ACCOUNTING

Made in the USA
Lexington, KY
29 March 2013